Keyboard Selections From The Messiah

Solos and Duets for Piano or Harpsichord

Arranged by Myra Schubert

CONTENTS

Lillenas PUBLISHING COMPANY
KANSAS CITY, MO 64141

Dedicated to Hannah Dedmon

For unto Us a Child Is Born

SECONDO

GEORGE FREDERICK HANDEL
Arranged by Myra Schubert

Dedicated to Abbie Dedmon

For unto Us a Child Is Born

PRIMO

GEORGE FREDERICK HANDEL
Arranged by Myra Schubert

Both hands one octave higher

Dedicated to Jan Laughlin

O Thou That Tellest Good Tidings to Zion

GEORGE FREDERICK HANDEL
Arranged by Myra Schubert

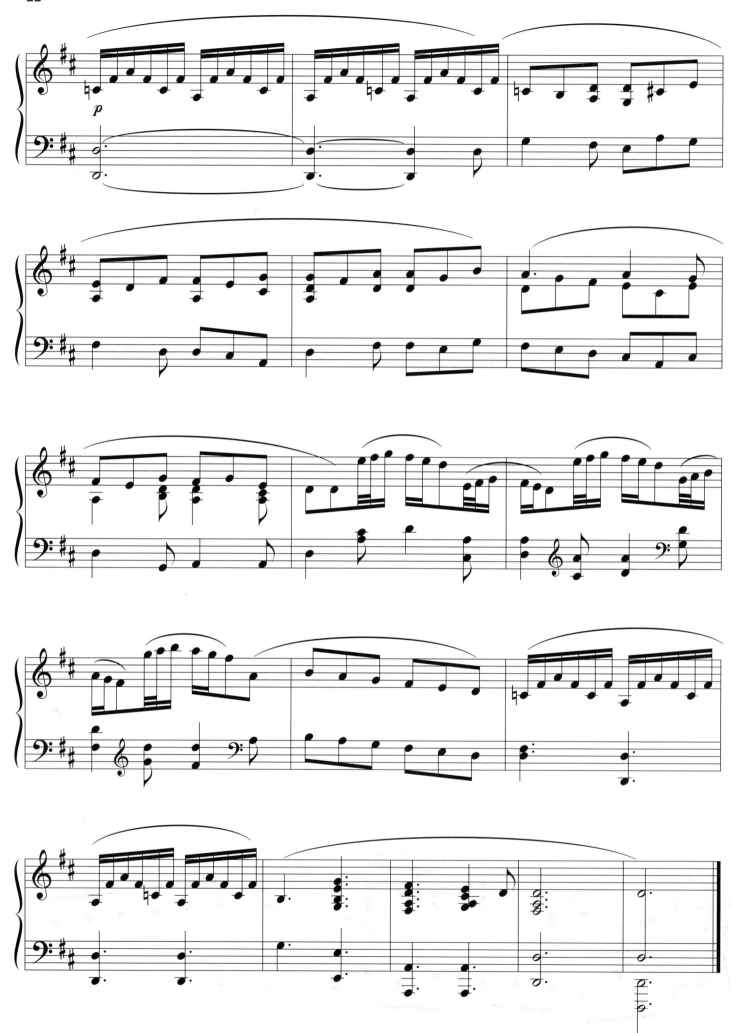

Dedicated to Brandon Cook

And the Glory of the Lord

GEORGE FREDERICK HANDEL
Arranged by Myra Schubert

Dedicated to Christy Ray

Glory to God

GEORGE FREDERICK HANDEL
Arranged by Myra Schubert

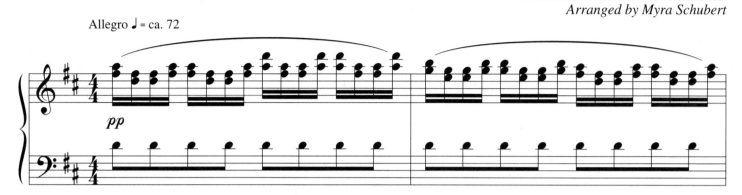

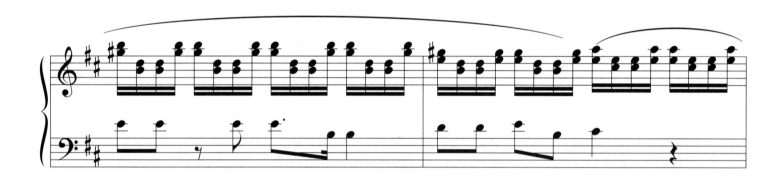

Dedicated to Erin McGarry

He Shall Feed His Flock

GEORGE FREDERICK HANDEL
Arranged by Myra Schubert

Larghetto e piano ♪ = ca. 112

Dedicated to Elizabeth Wilson

I Know That My Redeemer Liveth

GEORGE FREDERICK HANDEL
Arranged by Myra Schubert

Dedicated to Max Payne

Lift up Your Heads, O Ye Gates

GEORGE FREDERICK HANDEL
Arranged by Myra Schubert

This page is intentionally blank
to minimize page turns.

Dedicated to Aubrey Thompson

Hallelujah Chorus

SECONDO

GEORGE FREDERICK HANDEL
Arranged by Myra Schubert

Dedicated to Ashley Pitzer

Hallelujah Chorus
PRIMO

GEORGE FREDERICK HANDEL
Arranged by Myra Schubert

R. H. one octave higher

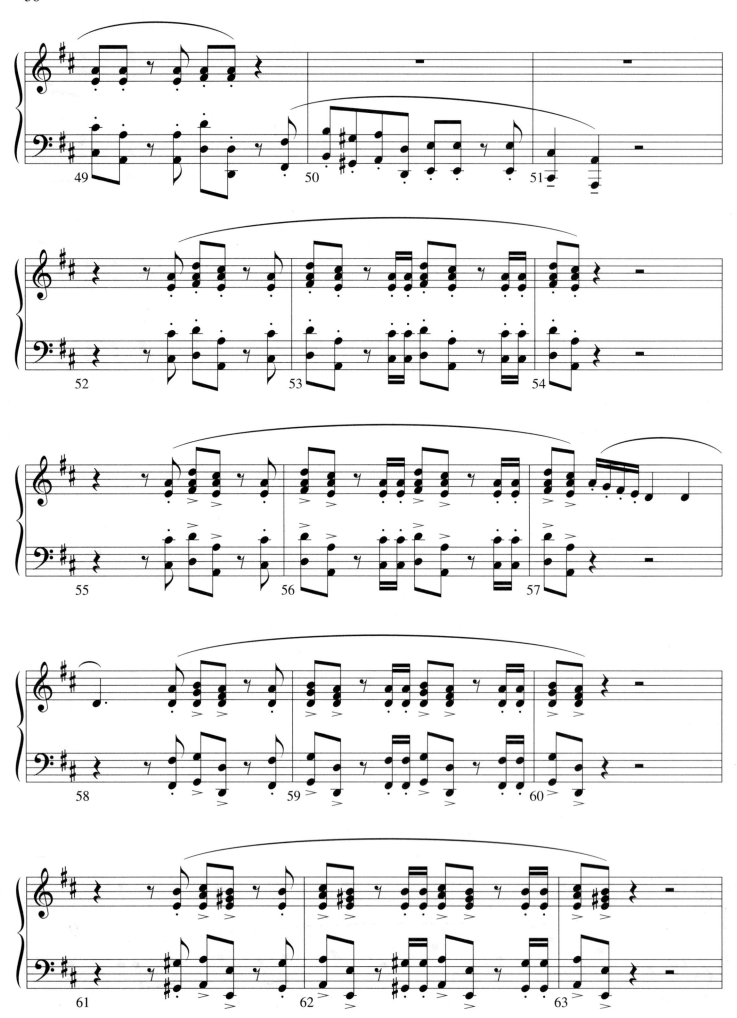

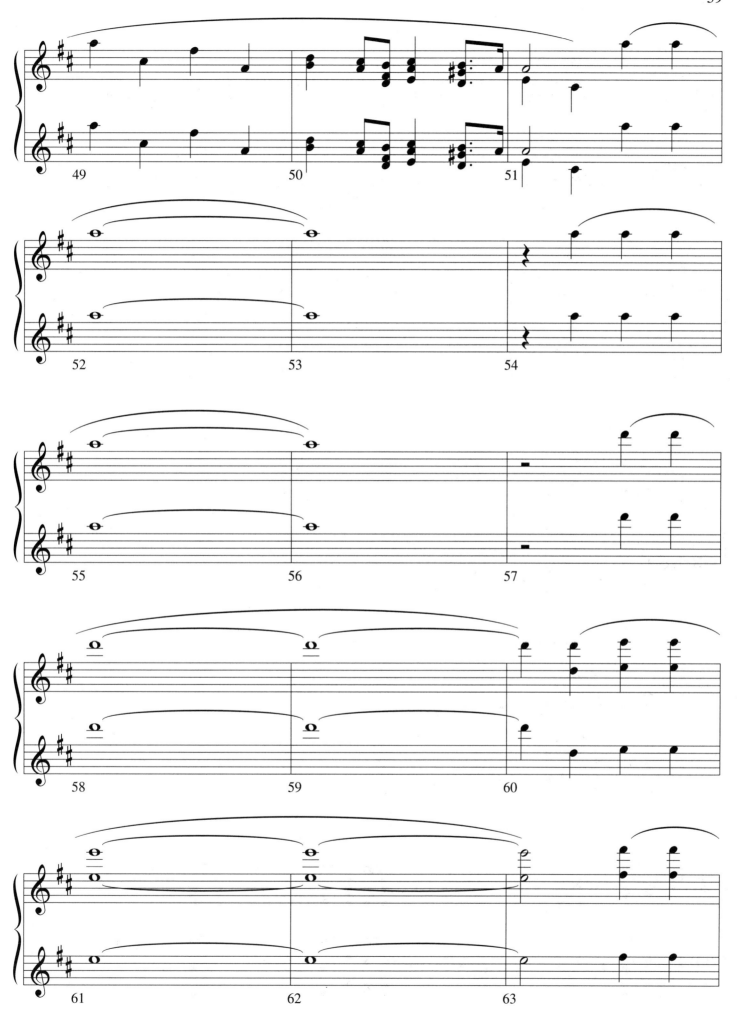